Landslide

poems by Andrew Jarvis

Landslide

poems by Andrew Jarvis

HOMEBOUND
PUBLICATIONS
Independent Publisher of Contemplative Titles
STONINGTON, CONNECTICUT

HOMEBOUND PUBLICATIONS
Ensuring the mainstream isn't the only stream.

For bulk ordering information or permissions write:
Homebound Publications, PO Box 1442
Pawcatuck, Connecticut 06379 United States of America

Visit us at: www.homeboundpublications.com

FIRST EDITION
ISBN: 978-1-938846-96-0 (pbk)

BOOK DESIGN
Front Cover Image: © Steve Carter
Cover and Interior Design: Leslie M. Browning

Library of Congress Cataloging-in-Publication Data

Names: Jarvis, Andrew, 1981- author.
Title: Landslide / by Andrew Jarvis.
Description: First edition. | Pawcatuck, Connecticut : Homebound
    Publications, 2016.
Identifiers: LCCN 2016028298 | ISBN 9781938846960 (pbk.)
Classification: LCC PS3610.A783 A6 2016 | DDC 811/.6—dc23
LC record available at https://lccn.loc.gov/2016028298

10 9 8 7 6 5 4 3 2 1

Homebound Publications holds a fervor for environmental conservation. Atop donating a percentage of our annual income to an ecological charity, we are ever-mindful of our "carbon footprint". Our books are printed on paper with chain of custody certification from the Forest Stewardship Council, Sustainable Forestry Initiative, and the Programme for the Endorsement of Forest Certification. This ensures that, in every step of the process, from the tree to the reader's hands, the paper our books are printed on has come from sustainably managed forests.

Landslide

poems by Andrew Jarvis

HOMEBOUND
PUBLICATIONS
Independent Publisher of Contemplative Titles
STONINGTON, CONNECTICUT

HOMEBOUND PUBLICATIONS
Ensuring the mainstream isn't the only stream.

For bulk ordering information or permissions write:
Homebound Publications, PO Box 1442
Pawcatuck, Connecticut 06379 United States of America

Visit us at: www.homeboundpublications.com

FIRST EDITION
ISBN: 978-1-938846-96-0 (pbk)

BOOK DESIGN
Front Cover Image: © Steve Carter
Cover and Interior Design: Leslie M. Browning

Library of Congress Cataloging-in-Publication Data

Names: Jarvis, Andrew, 1981- author.
Title: Landslide / by Andrew Jarvis.
Description: First edition. | Pawcatuck, Connecticut : Homebound
    Publications, 2016.
Identifiers: LCCN 2016028298 | ISBN 9781938846960 (pbk.)
Classification: LCC PS3610.A783 A6 2016 | DDC 811/.6—dc23
LC record available at https://lccn.loc.gov/2016028298

10 9 8 7 6 5 4 3 2 1

Homebound Publications holds a fervor for environmental conservation. Atop donating
a percentage of our annual income to an ecological charity, we are ever-mindful
of our "carbon footprint". Our books are printed on paper with chain of custody
certification from the Forest Stewardship Council, Sustainable Forestry Initiative, and
the Programme for the Endorsement of Forest Certification. This ensures that, in every
step of the process, from the tree to the reader's hands, the paper our books are printed
on has come from sustainably managed forests.

For Betty

Contents

Remains

Fissure

Scape

Remains

The Old House

At the beach of great fires, father
is burning our house into nails.

He deconstructed it, chopped it
with his long-handled axe, hacked it.

This is his frame of mind, unframed
while everything singes on sand.

His boards, his beams, his roof, his work,
he watches grandfather burning.

All of him lost in an hour,
he died building this house for us.

But father has a better build
with skylights and stairways in sun.

He paints us a picture with ash,
while grandfather peers through his smoke.

Blackberries

Grandfather is ripping
out all of her work, torn
from the roots, pierced berries
bleeding into black pools.

They were her covering,
the well of our ravine
blanketing juicy sweets,
to feed grandmother well.

She would battle her scars,
quilted in blackened skin,
as if she lost a war
to a thorny nightmare.

And she would dream of it,
the overkill of life
blooming like rising yeast,
the spread of growing seed.

Shaken, pulled at the stem,
shoveled for a sidewall,
this is the end of her
wonders, grandfather's weeds.

Gloves

He holds no leather,
        naked
like a lamb in snow,
        shivering.

He is unpaired, his fingers
        bare,
bruised like conifers,
        disbranched.

Nails stole his gloves,
        hammered
away, hidden under
        shingles.

No one will find them,
        lost
covers of the hammering
        man.

Concrete floor, cedar
        beams,
they warmed armed
        foundation.

Walls, heavy framed
       work,
were hoisted, hauled,
       placed.

We want to carry them,
       ascend
shingles to find the right
       fit.

Shot

He broke his everything
for it, to feel the deer,
his shotgun for hide.

Rabbits, pheasants, muskrats,
they eyed barrels of death,
metallic, merciless.

And he inhaled them
like a dead vortex,
siphoning rotten smell.

The learning of it, loss
in the sight of an aim,
he released aggression.

Like madness in a mind
shot into shrapnel thoughts,
he curtailed caliber.

And it is suffering,
bulleted and fallen,
pummeled for a life, purged.

The Nothing Bus

So this is where it stops,
between the fishmonger
and the forgotten walk,
the road where the dust clouds.

He has a reserved seat
next to the wooden post,
a cracked and dangling sign
for the forthcoming ones.

There will be a housewife
with a tacky top hat,
a nest made of roses,
a little lark within.

And she will have a son,
a proud and handsome one,
a smiling gifted child
who knows all the unknowns.

It will arrive on time,
as if a metronome
tick-tocks through the axles
and clocks his life for him.

He misses them again,
his nothings in the wind,
the ghosts who long passed by,
his drifters in the fog.

Buoy

She shovels his death dirt,
waking her sleeping son
with fresh forsythias.

Yellow, her beach beacon
shines, brightening her,
enlightening darkened.

In glow to salted eyes,
petals release pupils
from wet overpower.

He fell in this setting,
on a sailed shoreline,
dank drifter discovered.

A seaman silenced, drowned
in sea squall, overboard,
she dries him with flowers.

Seeded so stamens spout
the blood of him, he buds
in this buoy of blooms.

Father Haunts

So these are his voices,
the floating maniacs
of haunted memories.

They are inhumanly
loud like wild screech owls,
blaring sirens in night.

Father spoke of screamers,
spirits that pierce eardrums,
and we did not believe.

The warnings of the dead
sounding within the fog,
we run away from them.

Horses, piglets, and deer,
all the cries from the grave,
they smother us with sound.

Now remembering raw
tales of slaughtered ghosts,
we swallow his stories.

The Rod

The rod that reeks of fish.
The rod that came brand new.

The rod that confuses me.
The rod that you taught me with.

The rod that released a trout.
The rod that caught it.

The rod that I broke.
The rod that you fixed.

The rod that ate my flies.
The rod that casted them.

The rod that the creek hid.
The rod that you found.

The rod that I take fishing.
The rod that you gave me.

Sand Swimmer

He turns into new beach,
    rolling his age away, gray
sand swimmer cleaning in brine.

He picks all grained filth,
    revealing fresh white,
cleansing a birthed baby.

There will be an awakening,
    as if he burned in sun
to peel wrinkled skin.

It will be exhausting, ending
    anything evolved in pain,
like roses, prickles removed.

Then he rolls in water,
    wanting to wash away,
renewing life's wakes.

He dives in his eyes, smashes
    that monster in the mirror,
and glows among jellyfish.

The Boxes

There are even butterflies
with plastic cream and rose
wing clips, the colors fading
as if real porcelain.

The faux pearls have one,
the clasp rusted and weak
from all the tea parties
and a shortage of polish.

And one for the paperclips,
multicolored and divided
so each color has a space,
she refused to use staples.

She keeps a box for him
and all of his baseball cards,
a perfect hubby cubby
for all of his escapades.

She refilled the candy
when the grandchildren came,
peppermint mints and kisses
made of milk chocolate.

And we always found it,
in her special hiding place,
just below the pictures
and her little children things.

Cookie Jars

Grandmother died, and grandfather is gone,
away from this temple of temptation.

The kitty from Kyoto for blossoms,
cherries of a child, she remembers.

Juice dripping from her chin, as if bleeding,
she has a red boysenberry for that.

And a bicycle for all those lessons
and fractured ribs in emergency rooms,

its frame is painted in silver and white
to remember her father's arms, enrobed

beside a broken jalopy, a wreck
to recall her first parallel; they're parked.

There is even an educated owl
spelling the words of bees, as if a muse.

A bear with a bowtie, a crowned frog prince,
a coveted collection, it tempts touch.

So we open her ornate, ceramic
delicacies of life, shining, so sweet.

Exhibition

Just wait until the opening day,
when prehistoric undergrowth
will grow inside and live again.

She speaks of a mammoth on rocks,
its ivory tusks rounded and curved,
with an iceberg floating beside.

The woolly will be at center,
surrounded by interactive
nomads and animatronics.

And you will encounter a mist
seeping through the entrance, chilling
your face, making your eyebrows wave.

The grass, the ferns, the pine archway,
each little piece will have a place,
as shown on her exhibit map.

The design is so intricate,
quarantining spectacular,
like diamonds arranged under glass.

So she leaves everything empty
and draws dioramas in the air,
as if she is a saint of science.

Exhibit Screech

The reconstructed owl, no longer loud,
is stuffed like all things dead, with throat cotton
in a realistic setting, quiet.

Bending, the conditioned air is sounding
through its beak, a talkative movement,
as if captured in a turbulent stream.

The deaf boy listens, the exhibit howls
enticing him with its eloquent bird
like a muted sound mime speaking in air.

To the barrier, where the wall prevents
him from hypnotic notes, his ears yearning
to be pierced and hear its deafening screech.

Opening

There is a space for a jukebox
between the broken telephone
and jawbreaker vending machine.

She has never heard of the thing,
a player without a record
that pipes Elvis into the booths.

So she places the wood indian
in red headdress to sell cigars
to those who eat pie with their smoke.

And she has baked the apple ones
waiting for customers to slice
and taste the tree that grows outside.

She has polished the silverware
and plated the shortening to fry,
as if the eggs were preordered.

It is waiting for the switch flip
from off into on sparkling chrome,
ready for the first stool to break.

Hotel Puget

You can even buy the stairs,
with balusters blossoming
from rotten steps, the rails
stolen for shanties.

And the windows, you see
they are on sale; their frames
are free if you can use them
in a new kind of light.

There is a print of a parrot
perched on key limes,
as if it flew north with the fruit
to be stuffed for a stencil.

You can purchase the pillows,
complete with silk sheets,
an enrapture of memories
to blanket one's self.

And the organ, that ornate
blessing garnished with sound,
is for free, an unadvertised sale
with an entire outhouse.

Kimono

Blossoms, bamboo, and pine,
a crane poised on a tortoise,
they float with white and purple
rolling from the waist
down into whirlpools
at the knees.

They match the whiskers,
curled and elongated, they curve
just like the lips of the dead,
as if the robe had flown itself
over here from Japan
to haul away his seals.

He wonders if that lady,
the lanky one last night,
wants it returned, or if
she likes seafood. The wrap
fits around their flippers,
and he likes the color.

He will skin them for her,
squeeze out all the oil,
stew away the blubber,
then platter them unfurled
on that exotic dress, its symbols
meaning luck and longevity.

Fissure

Dry Season

This is the time of grandfather,
his wrinkled face cracked into mud
and drinking our river to dust.

He dries in the summer, its sun
making a well of him, drying
like a giant cork in our earth.

And he is laughing, his limestone
arranged in a smile, a grin
to gargle our water away.

He left us with raisins, berries
shriveled like our grandmother's skin,
restless, broken, and cackling.

We pray to water him, with storms
raining from our seasonal god,
flooding his body entire.

Pour down, grant us glaciers again;
we wait for you to rain your wet,
tap winter, and drown him in floe.

Rail Man

He has a twisted cane and strap
hoisting his busted leg and hip
burnt from the unforgiving steam.

His legs refuse to stand alone,
to strengthen a railway worker,
a broken man steaming upright.

And he speaks of the ties, the spikes
hammered into the railroad track,
blasted moments of derailment.

The ballast, anchor, and roadbed,
the torn unfastened fastenings,
they severed his whole to his parts.

He opens his pain, unfolding
his scarred fingers and fanning them,
digits dividing the mountains.

And then he traces a landslide,
a steep carving, plummeting slope,
a route where trains will roll, speeding.

Glass Plate Negative

Here is the firehouse,
its bell tower rising
before the great fire.

The ladder is shadowed
and leans against a rail,
three boys waving from it.

This is their last welcome,
with flames approaching them
like sparks to dynamite.

They did not hear it burn
or see someone set it,
like blind mice in earmuffs.

Smoldering bricks and shoes
untied without laces,
the ashes absorbed them.

And all of those horses,
the saddled responders,
they burned into rawhide.

This was their last capture,
the last living within
a negative city.

So trace the black outline
and picture their faces
that saw it in color.

Ghost Stairs

They rise in water spout
    where sea waves gargle
        and mud spews on itself,
           as if they sickened it.

Rigid and eternal,
    like bamboo in rainfall,
        they rise without splints
           into escaping day.

There were firemen,
    stepping upon the case,
        a stairway to heaven
           where rain poured freedom.

And there she rises,
    a girl to the vantage,
        to haunt the day,
           watching graveyard flood.

She outlines their faces,
    as if she has pencils
        attached to nails,
           sharpened to curve them.

A quirky mustache here,
    a careful forehead there,
        with wavy hair strands,
            she draws on everything.

Until moon rises,
    captures her cloaked,
        in intolerant white,
            she dies, beaming.

On the ghosts on the stairs,
    the men fallen aflame,
        they trap her on escape,
            burning for blessing.

Tornado

The uneasy oak is unwound
from the fingers of a twister,
like clay sculpted by whetted wind.

And the funnel has kissed the ground
in an angry suck with a smack
of rotational lips in storm.

By the windmill where the windows
are breaking into arrowheads,
a sparrow smothers the shingles.

Pressed there like garbage compacted,
its wings are tracing the trigger:
unequal winds in atmosphere.

Its feathers unfold in creases
and crush as if chewed by sky wolves
airborne, rabid, biting, aloft.

And its collide is caressing
the smothered siding, a canvas
of spread-eagled oil, awestruck.

Ruins

They squish their feet on the bottom,
the mud separating their toes
while slick oil encircles them.

These are the believers, lovers
of those highway off-ramps that stop
at walls without any exits.

College students and thrill seekers,
so many have dived in the dark,
plunging into ritual falls.

There is freedom among ruins,
those reinforced pillars rising
through space into time memories.

The waterway plastic, the rinds
of all those sweet watermelons,
the dead seabirds, they worship them.

Summer House

In summer, the walls slide away,
roll onto the rails above,
and sun embodies the living.

It transforms like a music box
waiting to be opened, its sound
unleashed when the sides are unhinged.

And they welcome us in light tones,
those porcelain dogs and the ship
sailing away in its bottle.

Her corner loom, her wedding gown,
grandfather's collection of cars;
we must admire their polish.

And then we see china, roses
around the edges, with berries
embossed on pearl platters, brimming.

Grandmother arranged this setting,
ornate, so that everything shined,
so we would admire the work.

Warm Rain

When rain refused blankets, and clouds
began to burn like charred paper,
we discovered that fire could fly.

It can flutter between cedars
like butterflies among daises,
ever so peaceful and floating.

Sunflowers and cattle, horses
unable to canter to cold,
you cannot extinguish the hot.

So this is how nature removes
everything from the outside in,
from forests to floorboards, burning.

The crimson dancers of the hours,
we flame and surrender to you,
dreaming of pours, the falling rain.

Come sky, wrap us in rainfall,
blanket us in your water drops,
the little robes of wet, warming.

Night Flight

The watchmen envision a wake,
something before the moon rises,
quickly causing enlightenment.

They saw a sail last night, a wave
of air turning its direction,
but they remained there unwavered.

And the whale calls are old music,
the pitches sounding on flat ears
that hear the ordinary night.

But then they hear a shattering,
as if the sky was breaking glass,
a thunder without lightening.

It blinks like a bolting firefly
determined to light up the night,
beaming with supersonic sound.

So they warn it, reach for its wings
to break them before it reaches
the seawall, forcing its stop.

Then it passes, that thunderbird
refusing to slow in their sight,
enraging those with blinded eyes.

Within the Mudslide

We found a creation,
a totem pole carving
of salmon under earth.

The cedar spawns its eyes,
circles enchanting us
to recall an elder.

He must have swum oceans
like quick sockeye feeding
on lice and dragonflies.

And he built it, this lodge
emerging through the slide,
to smoke fish on alders.

And it is enormous,
as if he drained the sea
to fortify its planks.

So we reconstruct it
and all of his totem,
resurrecting his tale.

Goodbye, Wave

Entrails in sea air,
  livers absorbing lice,
it smells of woven death.

Expired milk and mold
  encrusting stale loaves,
they roll in spoiled roe.

With cartons waving by,
  we welcome the wasted
fragments of fermented.

The ornamental fruit
  glossy in oiled glaze,
it shimmers like ice, flossed.

Seagulls walk on water,
  along with drifting rats;
it is our masterpiece.

Propelled by water's way,
  we wave goodbye our art,
soured and set, sailing.

The Demon

She will appear in the spillage,
in the slick of a whale

woven by the shore scavengers
pecking over the entrails.

She is the demon, the mother
of midnight oil in moonlight.

Her eyes are like splinters, piercing
explorers who seek out her sheen.

And she will eat you entire,
if you discuss her saliva.

One day we discover a dead,
a humpback oozing her magic.

So we sacrifice fat to it,
dispelling her, adorning brave.

Encampment

They need the dead, the drifts
of wood and timber chopped
from top to bottom today.

It is an aquatic puzzle, the pieces
unfit for homes but rising, houses
made of twigs and watered dust.

A plan of deliberate pimples,
they mound in ordered brown,
as if the bluff has oily skin.

It will be a city of carvings,
with rooftops made of redwoods
unearthed to top moldings.

And there will be berries
like blue and red fireworks
booming in ripe blooms.

So slice through the current
and raise water logs; the stems
need you to imagine the fruit.

Oil Bears

Albinos over the oil,
white bears contrast the black, wild
and sleeping above the shale.

Unprotected over the rich,
a rare ocean of wealth, they sleep
on a midnight tap, then a spout.

A pipeline will blacken their fur
and flow through enchanted forests
like witch fingers casting a spell.

In a hibernation of silt,
bears will burrow in ancient gold,
too bright for a bargain, enriched.

Refined and flowing, they observe
their rainforest drilling away,
in awe of the steep of the sheen.

Just imagine the slick of it,
a carnivorous way, carving
a byway of bones for life's crude.

Awakened Art

The bears are not hibernating,
black sleepwalkers digging through sand.

They chew the beach like wood chippers,
suck the grains, then spit out the stones.

They are the movers, the mammals
that descend at night, unbridled.

They toss over the drifted wood
and search for the living in dead.

And they will devour the life,
all night crawlers and geoducks.

There will be no fasting, no fish
released from their ravenous drools.

And like a graveyard at sunrise,
you see the lumped tombs in morning.

The sun reflects wild sculptures,
the clawed art of the awakened.

Consumed

The salmon smoke bellowed,
and cedars uprooted,
when land slid into earth.

And she swallowed herself
when the sunken longhouse
folded within the fog.

The carvings of fathers,
the unwoven weavings,
it unraveled their art.

Into absence, the home
of all the gatherings,
she framed it for nothing.

So this is consumption,
when ground opens its mouth
and chews all its covers.

It steals your hunger,
takes your cravings away,
and leaves you digested.

The Crawl

Father drew a constellation
and threw it over a mountain.

      He formed a whale with his fingers,
      an orca jumping over waves.

The body curved over the nails,
with tail from index to the thumb.

      This is how you slice the water,
      the stroke cutting, the legs in tow.

The river starts at the summit
and dives as fast as the killer.

      And you can be that swift, like falls
      sprinting away from glacial ice.

So curl your hands like the dorsal
and learn to crawl within the clouds.

Thunderbird

He shouts thunder up stream
from his dark Elwha cave
to chase salmon away
with lightning from his wings.

He has planted a fish
so large that we will wear
its bones as white jewelry
and feed its skin to fires.

It will be swimming soon,
spawning before our feet,
so grab the net and wait
for his great fins to surge.

But our firebird has lost,
losing our storm to sun,
the gray and black to bright
yellows and golds of day.

And so we seek his sound,
the high return of him
to storm the stream with fish,
creating a feast from flight.

Hatch

This is a last meal,
plated on a wingtip,
seasoned for the sly fox.

Too hungry to drop drool,
he slurps his saliva
to sense the taste of her.

He eats through her ceiling,
a fox biting the whole
of her, halving her wings.

He rips them for newborns,
the plumpest ones, too ripe
for anyone but him.

She watches him ravage
egg after egg, the orbs
awakened and shell shocked.

Not frenzied, she feels
like an urchin in sea,
sunken, baiting his bite.

She kills, clawing his eyes,
blinding him for rebirth,
cozy, covered in fur.

The Sharp Fox

Is restless within red,
a watchman enlivened
by magnetic land move,
it is shaken, alarmed.

Then something awakens,
stirring the soothsayer,
like a seizure of thought
convulsing in sky shake.

A mouse, perhaps, mundane
and peeking on prairie,
it could be a boring,
forsaken by sharp fox.

It unfurls to unwound
to find a formation,
focused within its sight,
the eye of a shotgun.

It shoots silent to loud,
a shock, a blow, fired
into thinking, ears pierced;
it parts its head to halves.

Epiphany somehow
seizes within the split,
dull thoughts sharpened in death:
a man, alive, in blood.

Dam Ladder

See how they open their eyes wide,
the watchers of the waterfall,
motionless and scared of its speed.

It is a constant fall, timing
and running away with the dead,
as if a great watch erupted.

The unhooked trout, the shot eagle,
even a beaver unable
to build its water wall, they drowned.

And it is pooling around them,
as hours die under the flood,
rising into enormity.

So they will dam it, break the time
with a concrete ladder, stepping
over each death into ages.

Dam Overlook

It is an angry earth,
but nobody believed
it could crumble concrete.

It cracked in an earthquake
that crippled the high wall,
shaken, broken, unfixed.

She prepares for a pour
that bursts when a storm cloud
cries like an eye, piercing.

A dreamer on the dam,
feathering wind, she learns
the lift of an eagle.

To be like her great bird,
she glides over the falls,
survives when water breaks.

Unbound, airborne, at ease,
she rises in redwoods,
watching pools overflow.

River Life

Red runs like ink on a soft hand,
its fingers slicing mountain tops
and falling into colored skin.

This is a river of salmon
spawning water babies in roe,
spherical birth in fish scales.

Overflowing by water's edge,
we feel the surface, rolling
our fingers in radiant waves.

As smooth as a ruby's façade,
we shine in their enlightenment,
the wet faces of river flow.

And we learn of life in color,
remembering those bloody hands
pulsing, glowing, thriving, in spawn.

Catch and Release

We found a new floater,
a bird bound in a line
we left for the fishes.

It had a mummy moan
like helium hissing
into a white balloon.

Its beak was like a clamp
pressing in on itself,
too tight to unravel.

And its wings were mangled,
meant to soar but shredded
in our ultra-thin line.

Threads were without mercy,
braided and spun to crack
like whips in stormy sky.

Encaged within our crate,
we watched it slowly die,
rolling, pulsing to death.

Until we cast it off,
released it in water,
to float as our new fly.

The Fishery

The broken window panes
point at each other, glass
blades slicing through sea air,
monuments for gutters.

It is a gathering,
of traps and fishing lines,
of shredded wood oarlocks,
of watered memories.

And sea lions adore
the abandoned, the thawed
freezers of heads and tails,
as if they found Eden.

They weigh themselves on scales,
balancing on flippers,
rolling through the decayed,
the heavy afterthoughts.

One catches a crawler,
a crab breaking through pots,
a king escaping jail
and caught by a crabber.

It was the last living
ornament in this house
eaten while lions growl
into eternity.

Scrimshaw

He picks up the tusk and turns it,
in awe of her finely carved eyes
and hair curving to catch the wind.

The walrus must have died near here,
hunted by her artist and speared
to capture her in ivory.

The neck, the jaw, the face, the ears,
they flow like a fast waterfall
caressing the slope with its slide.

He wants to render her again,
feel what it means to be perfect,
to paint the delicate in white.

So he will hunt out a new beast,
cut off its head and steal its tusks,
to carve out the beauty from it.

Weaving a Man

At the place of the bitter roots,
where fireflies descend and rise,
a weaver is working cedar.

She peeled the bark off the back
of the overturned red nearby,
where dead ends resemble wrinkles.

She says a man is there, his face
like squid chili with wooden legs
and tentacles warping the hairs.

Today he is inviting her
to pry off his skin and sew it
into blankets of fibrous twill.

And she accepts, as if his weight
grabbed her into the ground, sank her
to enliven the undergrowth.

She remakes the patchwork of him,
a brocade of earth embodied,
the strands of an interlaced man.

Crawlers

They squirm like snakes on Medusa, sliming
in glorious death where everything grows
for the grave boy dissecting with switchblade.

He slices them, rearranges their heads,
and wraps their bodies like rings, so shiny
in the moonlight, a monarch of the worms.

Lost in fluctuation of overflow,
he reaches into detritus, the deep
pulse of land pushing against fingerprints.

Jarring, he screws the mason lid tightly
to tell his tale to mother, her call
sounding like a shrieking owl, maddening.

She defines the unmoved, no nightwalker
or woman under new moon; she believes
in bacteria, and that all things bite.

So he will show her, present them to her
like a gift to a shrew, taming, so sick.
They become her disease; she baited it.

Goose

This is a prize, plated
    so wings spread
       the way it flew
         when falling.
It bolted, inverted
    like lightening
       striking sky, silver
         lining its wings, black
rounding its breast
    into target.
       With one gun
         point, the thrill
was in gawk, the sound
    of shooting, family
       listening on; he sounded
         wild in free range.
A sonic boom,
    bloody, it is organic,
       crisp like red rain
         rewarding his cleft;
he sucks sharp.

Above Juneau

There is a certain light
waving above Juneau,
captured in his album

of everything wrangled,
disemboweled, and stuffed;
he was a true hunter.

Of deer, of bears, and all
the living in wild,
he shot in amazement.

Then evergreen found him,
fluorescent and dangling
like icicles on jade.

Green glided over red
and ran his rage away;
he focused on the shine,

the sheer floating of it,
alive while he let life
enliven and shimmer.

North had broken the man
into a new dreamer,
and he had to shoot it.

Scape

Old Growth

Grandfather grew forests for us,
pierced the clouds and summoned their falls,
feeding the roots of his children.

And he grew us in evergreens,
measured our limbs by long branches,
our teeth by the points of needles.

He spoke of redwoods and old growth,
saying we will grow forever
like tree arrows shooting to sky.

But his was misfired and burned
in a fire without flooding,
swallowing him without a storm.

He rose into ancestral smoke,
joining the ashes of elders,
to learn of a life without rain.

So we pour over him, reading
his ages, the teachings of rings,
each one remembering water.

Snow Flower

Among the midwinter fire,
daylight is gilding arms.

They rise into its gold,
a bright planting of red.

In white, matting the ground,
they thrive from its feeding.

They fall under shadow,
the vision of a man

searching for life in things,
gardening in the sun.

And fertilizing growth,
he embodies their blaze.

He does not grow in snow,
but rather earth, flaming.

Daffodils

She speaks of a poison, unpretending
to plant perennials that bloom for life.

Daffodils, they catalyze the demise
of moles, of rabbits, of the ravenous.

They eat the earth below, their bulbs bigger
than lilies, poppies, as if layered lords.

They die badly, so she embodies them,
plotting each bulb to blossom in yellow.

To live in light, growing in a garden
gifted to them, to tease all the tulips.

And like a funeral planner, she plants
her hands in sick soil, feeling undead.

Preserves

Grandmother has apples across
the grimace of souring lips,
the sweets of her only orchard
burning in grandfather's fire.

Vibrant, the view of it flaming
like pitchforks skewering sunlight,
then erupting mouthfuls of ash
into the wet mouth of a wife.

White, his favorite bread, and butter,
he doesn't like jelly—the gel
is too oozy, so she swallows
the preference of him, the cream.

Into a waterfall, her work
will run away with delicious,
a golden realm with pectin mulch
and blooming lilies, without juice.

Monument

The wood of the wheelbarrow, too dead
to deliver any bushel of brush,
is orgasmic, enlivened by lichen.

She pushed it here, exhausted her muscle
to build fires in days burning to nights;
a monument to her work, it blazes

a lush embellishment of evergreen
bodies, as if colonized by cosmic
orbs of gas, atmospheric and blooming.

White and green seep into yellow, then black
bursts along the wooden plane, where her hands
held onto color, the crimson handles

of years decomposing in parasites,
symbiotic, breathing, biologic;
in her afterlife, they grip, and thrive.

Forager

Horsetails and knotweed,
the bases of bitters,
she speaks of sustenance.

She grapples them, as if
overgrowth had opened
a gastronomic gate.

Overgrown weed woman
eating dandelions
and all, she salivates.

Obsessed, ingredients
otherwise invasive,
she picks palatables.

It is a beckoning,
to differ their demise,
and she will boil them.

The greens, even the browns
will live an afterlife,
embodied within broth.

And all too nutritious
to kill our annoyance,
she stings, watching us starve.

Memory Bird

It must have flown from her secret garden,
where sunflowers turned with rising sunrays,
her special castle moat protecting it.

Its feathers are awkward and exposing
a round belly seeded by her feedings,
as if it died waiting for its next meal.

She sees where it escaped her hideaway,
a tiny scar running from eye to beak,
where life unwrapped, unruffled, unfolded.

And like an architect drafting the air,
she wants to remodel her memories,
piece together the wings, and fly back home.

Bulldozer

There go the camellias,
their roly-poly pinks
peeling like sunburnt skin.

> And the rhododendrons
> roll into sewer blooms,
> a ripening of red.

This is architecture,
the plans for a mansion
rising on bulldozed bulbs.

> Dream of it, a building
> over the blooming dead,
> built by an erasure.

It will glisten and glow
within a housed heaven,
awake after a doze.

> Live in it, dwell on death
> and all of its flowers,
> and watch the garden roll.

The Feeling

The farm is growing fur, rotten,
with animals sprouting, living,
as if mud became a mammal.

Flooded into mole spout, they spread
over our field like a throw
of woven hair plucked from earth's scalp.

Beaten brown, streaked in red, our hands
reach into suffocated soft
comforters, hides of watered hills.

So sinful, the feel of skin
kissing our fingers, the oozing
massage, it is a fatty spa.

Pulling water pelts, we clear them
to plant new seed, as if the rain
swept pests to fertilize with death.

To burn after flood, we fire
everything furry, unfurling
their flesh, making pelleted feed.

Mercury Dive

Just wait until it frosts the eaves,
when the wind will unwind and freeze
on all the awls, even the oil.

The swallows are silent, the owls
absent from the rickety roof,
but the crying have taken aloft.

The membranes, the digits, the tips,
bat wings unfolded and flapping,
they swarm like blinded butterflies.

And maybe the barn will buckle,
collapse like a sinkhole of sludge
unbothered by flimsy abodes.

So welcome the mercury dive
and pray that those pitches will drop,
the notes flattened, frozen, silenced.

Termites

The termites have rooted
wood weavings underground,
the twisted fruit of earth
rotting above, bitten.

The knots, the burls, the bark
taken by constant bites
like analog molars
chipping away at time.

Its hours are numbered,
this log broken, upright
and born from a redwood
that fell within the fall.

Capture this dying art,
while everything accounts
to the hours, unbound
by cleaners of life's core.

Heart Rot

Essential to the evergreen,
it eats into the heart of it.

Roosting, resting in its hollow,
it wastes into thrive, eternal.

Like a neutron bomb, blossoming,
it blooms into a mushroom cloud.

Fungus, it bites through decayed burls
afoul within a Douglas fir.

It kills, as if a black widow
under a veil of bark lace.

Living, it causes crucial death,
for coniferous feed, for life.

And so it pulses into rot,
the blood of the forest, bleeding.

Pollination

A colony of bees
has captured our garden,
yellow and black, the grass
no longer painted green.

They move pollen in plants,
disarranging arranged
blossoms of sunflowers,
a golden formation

waving this way, that way,
bumbling their juicy buds
while they buzz around rows,
not caring much for mulch.

Mother warned us of this,
nature's careful design
pollinating the world,
our pests withdrawing pulp.

And if we erase them,
leaving their bumbles parched,
life would stop coloring
the whites of our winters.

Web Queen

She rises at sunrise
to find woven night webs
reflecting morning light.

They quiver like touched skin,
cold and ready to wrap
around a warm lover.

She is bound in their weaves,
a web-walker enrobed
in silver, delicate.

They spin on forever,
a labyrinth of floss
enticing enchantment.

Poisoned, preying on her,
black creatures with venom,
they bite with tinctured fangs.

So she will be their queen
with an arachnid crown,
unleashed, smitten with crawls.

Hive Mind

She shatters for its soft
comb, a slugger for ooze,
like an awful creature
seeking a drink of death's
gold, a beaten honey.

Like an airy seizure,
she is shaking the wind
with her wooden bee bat,
silencing the buzzing
to taste their succulence.

Stings enrapture her arms
in this fog of yellow
and black, the pheromones
of bicolor coma;
she fights color to sleep.

In that cover of taste,
that woven quilt of hive,
she bludgeons to golden,
bloody bees for a suck
of sugar on her tongue.

Now this is wealth, a girl
standing on gore, gifted
the fruits of the flowers
flooding her sugared mouth,
pleasing, porous, so sweet.

Deaf Caps

She caresses the white city,
its walls welcoming the seekers

of solace, away from all sound;
she pulses in its pleasure domes.

No one would wonder of poison
in peace, as if at war with cries.

Not even a dreamer as deaf
as calm, but she had a thought.

In the silence, that great nothing
veiling her ears, it softens.

Like cotton absorbing cloud bursts,
the mushrooms are sounding divine.

Rising, a heaven of spores, pierced,
she carefully kisses the caps.

Digesting their deliciousness,
the umami of death, she owns

their oral umbrella, the off
of everything loud; she mutes life.

Biology

The formaldehyde frog
is enlivening her
with a scent of sour.

It is mother inside,
breathing behind the tongue,
swimming in its bladder.

She steeps in the red spleen,
circulating in blood,
birthing in rotten eggs.

They were our garden gore,
where amphibians fell
to her furious rake.

Their legs in our lilies
glowed like erupted jade,
graceless, awful, acute.

And she is wide open,
residing in the lobes;
she must have murdered it,

made its heart stop beating
for us to open death,
dissecting her divine.

Acknowledgements

"The Old House" *Measure: A Review of Formal Poetry*

"Father Haunts" *Poets Are Present Anthology*, Shakespeare Theater Company

"The Rod" *Ascent*, Finishing Line Press

"The Boxes" *Ascent*, Finishing Line Press

"Exhibition" *Westward Quarterly*

"Opening" *San Pedro River Review*

"Rail Man" *Valparaiso Poetry Review*

"Tornado" *Ginosko Literary Journal*

"Warm Rain" *Evansville Review*

"Within the Mudslide" *Appalachian Heritage*

"Encampment" *Soundings Review*

"Consumed" *Tulane Review*

"River Life" *Wildness: Voices of the Sacred Landscape Anthology*, Homebound Publications

"The Fishery" *Freshwater*

"Crawlers" *Ginosko Literary Journal*

"Snow Flower" *Westview*

"Daffodils" *Fractal Literary Magazine*

"Monument" *Inscape*

"The Feeling" *Permafrost*

"Pollination" *James Dickey Review*

"Hive Mind" *Ginosko Literary Journal*

"Deaf Caps" *Illuminations*

"Biology" *Cottonwood*

About the Author

Andrew Jarvis is the author of *Sound Points* (Red Bird Press), *Ascent* (Finishing Line Press), and *The Strait* (Homebound Publications). His poems have appeared in *Cottonwood, Evansville Review, Valparaiso Poetry Review, Tulane Review,* and several other magazines. He was a Finalist for the 2014 Homebound Publications Poetry Prize, and he has been a Finalist for two INDIEFAB Book of the Year Awards. He is also on the editorial board of Red Dashboard LLC. Andrew holds an M.A. in Writing (Poetry) from Johns Hopkins University.

HOMEBOUND PUBLICATIONS

Ensuring that the mainstream isn't the only stream.

At Homebound Publications, we publish books written by independent voices for independent minds. Our books focus on a return to simplicity and balance, connection to the earth and each other, and the search for meaning and authenticity. Founded in 2011, Homebound Publications is one of the rising independent publishers in the country. Collectively through our imprints, we publish between fifteen to twenty offerings each year. Our authors have received dozens of awards, including: *Foreword Reviews'* Book of the Year, Nautilus Book Award, Benjamin Franklin Book Awards, and Saltire Literary Awards. Highly-respected among bookstores, readers and authors alike, Homebound Publications has a proven devotion to quality, originality and integrity.

We are a small press with big ideas. As an independent publisher we strive to ensure that the mainstream is not the only stream. It is our intention at Homebound Publications to preserve contemplative storytelling. We publish full-length introspective works of creative non-fiction as well as essay collections, travel writing, poetry, and novels. In all our titles, our intention is to introduce new perspectives that will directly aid humankind in the trials we face at present as a global village.

WWW.HOMEBOUNDPUBLICATIONS.COM

Printed in the USA
CPSIA information can be obtained
at www.ICGtesting.com
JSHW080005150824
68134JS00021B/2288